Sunrise Over South Africa

Sunrise Over South Africa

Poems by

Joseph Kuhn Carey

© 2026 Joseph Kuhn Carey. All rights reserved.
This material may not be reproduced in any form, published,
reprinted, recorded, performed, broadcast,
rewritten or redistributed without
the explicit permission of Joseph Kuhn Carey.
All such actions are strictly prohibited by law.

Cover design by Shay Culligan
Cover image by Joseph, Renata, Joey, and Nicholas Carey
Author photo by Renata Carey

ISBN: 978-1-63980-996-7
Library of Congress Control Number: 2025951561

Kelsay Books
502 South 1040 East, A-119
American Fork, Utah 84003
Kelsaybooks.com

*for Renata, Joey, and Nicholas
and much-missed Mom, Dad, and Diane*

South Africa is the most beautiful place on earth. Admittedly, I am biased but when you combine the natural beauty . . . and the fact that the region is a haven for Africa's most splendid wildlife . . . then I think that we have been blessed with a truly wonderful land.
—Nelson Mandela

You have to understand—there is a romance to Africa. You can see a sunset and believe you have witnessed the hand of God. You watch the slow lope of a lioness and forget to breathe. You marvel at the tripod of a giraffe bent to water. In Africa, there are iridescent blues on the wings of birds that you do not see anywhere else in nature. In Africa, in the midday heat, you can see blisters in the atmosphere. When you are in Africa, you feel primordial, rocked in the cradle of the world.
—Jodi Picoult, *Leaving Time*

When you have caught the rhythm of Africa, you find out that it is the same in all her music.
—Karen Blixen, *Out of Africa*

Acknowledgments

Gratitude to the following journals, anthologies, and organizations, which chose the following poems for awards and publication, in print and online:

Collection Awards
(As a Manuscript)

London Book Festival (April 2024): Winner, "Poetry" Category; 2nd Place Winner, "Wild Card" Category
New York Book Festival (August 2024): Runner-Up Award, "Poetry" Category
Paris Book Festival (September 2024): Runner-Up Award, "Poetry" Category; Runner-Up Award, "Travel" Category
San Francisco Book Festival (June 2024): Runner-Up Award, "Poetry" Category

Individual Poem Awards

93rd Annual Writer's Digest Writing Competition (2024): "The Good Driver" received an Honorable Mention Award in the Non-Rhyming Poetry Category
Highland Park Poetry (2019): "Puffs of Smoke" was nominated for a Pushcart Prize Award
Illinois State Poetry Society Poetry Contest (2018): "Dance Party at the Durban Airport" was selected as a First-Place Winner in the "Giving Voice" Category

Publication

Distilled Lives, Volume 7 (Illinois State Poetry Society, 2024): "Golf in the Sunshine," "The Cape Point Lighthouse"

East on Central (2022, 2023, 2025): "Cleopatra's Needle," "The Africa Café," "Touching the Waters"

Highland Park Poetry: "The Ostriches of Oudtshoorn," "The Glassblowers of Eswatini," "A Tower of Giraffes," "Two Lane Road," "The Hot Towel," "Puffs of Smoke"

Illinois State Poetry Society: "A Hamburger at Woolworths," "Cable Car to Table Mountain," "Head in the Clouds," "The African Drum"

Inkwell (Decatur Area Poets, 2024): "Giraffes on the Run," "The Potholes at Bourke's Luck"

Road Trips (Highland Park Poetry, 2024): "Two Lane Road"

Contents

Author's Note	15
Invitation to an Adventure	19
Sardines by the Gate	21
Eleven Languages	22
The Big Bronze Bears	23
So Many Screens	24
The Hot Towel	25
A Hamburger at Woolworths	26
Nelson Mandela's Home	28
The African Drum	29
The Soul of Soweto	30
The Bright Light	31
Monkeys in the Fields	32
The Potholes at Bourke's Luck	33
Canyons on the Curves	34
A Formidable Combination	35
A Tower of Giraffes	36
The Lioness	37
The Hyena Pups	38
A Dazzle of Zebras	39
Wind Whipping Through the Safari Jeep	40
Giraffes on the Run	41
The Bathroom Attendant	42
Sunrise Over South Africa	43
Two Poachers	44
The Macadamia Nut Man	45
Harrie's Pancakes	46
South Africanisms	47
Zulu Wedding Dance	49
A Piece of Chocolate	50
Woman Under a Curved Tree	52

The Glassblowers of Eswatini	53
The Operatic Dinner Singer	54
Two Lane Road	55
I Blew the Fuse	56
Braai	59
Searching for Hippos	60
Elephants and Dirt	61
Feet to the Fire	62
The Gurgling Drain	63
The Peace of the Rolling Road	64
The Mountains of South Africa	65
Baboons on the Road	66
Swimming in South Africa	67
Touching the Waters	69
Dance Party at the Durban Airport	70
Indian Ocean Sun	72
The Waves and the Mouth	73
The Knysna Fires	74
The Knysna Seahorse	76
Talking to My Sons	77
The Shantytowns	78
Cars on the Wrong Side of the Road	79
Wind Turbines Turning Slowly	80
Cleopatra's Needle	81
The Ostriches of Oudtshoorn	83
The Aloe Tree	84
The Soup in Swellendam	85
Rugby, Cricket, Soccer	86
The Average South African Has Never Seen Snow	87
Head in the Clouds	88
The Tree Canopy Walk in the Garden	89
The Company's Garden	90

The Africa Café	91
The Man in the Van	92
The Good Driver	94
A Round at the Royal Cape Golf Club	96
Golf in the Sunshine	97
The Stone Masons	98
Dinner in a South African Home	100
Cable Car to Table Mountain	102
So Many Casks	103
The Southwesternmost Point of the African Continent	104
The Cape Point Lighthouse	105
The Flying Dutchman	106
The African Penguins at Boulders Beach	108
Puffs of Smoke	109
Traveling with My Sons	110
The Beauty of the Far, Far Away	112
A Diamond in the Sun	113

Author's Note

What a joy it was to travel to South Africa with my wife Renata, and then sixteen-and-fourteen-year-old sons, Joey and Nicholas, for almost three weeks in the summer of 2017. For my sons, who would both eventually become Eagle Scouts, it was the "scouting" adventure trip of a lifetime, including several incredible safari rides (featuring up-close visits with giraffes, lions, hyenas, elephants, impalas, kudus, elands, springboks, baboons, monkeys, hippos, rhinos, crocodiles and water buffaloes), as well as visits to mountain caves, Zulu villages, ostrich farms, bustling large cities, a tiny country with a king, oceans, savannas, botanic gardens, South African family homes, and beaches full of penguins. Every day on our zig-zag cross-country path from Johannesburg on the east to Cape Town on the west there were always new, exciting sights to be seen, voices to be heard, and memories to be made.

In addition, due to the fact that Wi-Fi, internet, and cell phone connections were often unavailable or a bit erratic (except in some hotel lobbies), we had the chance to break free from social media, calls, and internet surfing searches and pay close attention to the amazing landscapes and experiences surrounding us together as a family. By tackling such a vast country over a longer trip period of three weeks, we were also able to absorb more of this fascinating and diverse culture and learn about the horrific evils of Apartheid, the long fight for freedom and democracy and the struggles of a newly-birthed nation to find its proper way in the world.

It was also a revelation to discover how deeply South Africans admire and love Nelson Mandela. Each day, the leader of our tour would walk the bus aisles (as we rolled through the countryside and stopped in small & large towns) to tell us stories about his beloved country and provide us with special Nelson Mandela sayings and quotes. And what wonderful, meaningful, and memorable words they were! It was as if this one awe-inspiring freedom fighter, leader, and world figure had somehow encapsulated the meanings and goals of life, love, family, friends and government in spectacular and gripping short sentences that always made you think, reflect, and change. My sons wrote down a number of these heart-and-mind-touching sayings and quotes and many of them are included here throughout this book of travel poems.

Through these quotes and, hopefully, also my poems, I believe that you'll be able to experience a bit of South Africa and see why it's one of the most breathtaking places to visit in the world. South Africa is a truly spectacular place, an endless colorful quilt of peoples, cultures, sights and sounds, and our trip through it was unforgettable. Each day, we couldn't wait for the sun to come up again and shed light on wonderful and often astounding new things to see, and I will always cherish my time with my family there.

Lastly, this book could not have been written without the support, love and laughter of my wife and sons, who have been, and always will be, my treasured travel companions. This book is for them and anyone who wishes to see the world and grow and change as the faraway adventures of a lifetime unfurl like a magic carpet, beckoning you to step aboard, open your eyes & heart, and come willingly along for the exhilarating ride.

—Joseph Kuhn Carey

Invitation to an Adventure

Joseph Kuhn Carey invites the reader on an adventure to South Africa—to open their senses to its magical landscapes, wildlife, hospitality, and friendliness of its people.

As a South African reader, I appreciated how accurate the author's observations were and how well he received the positive attitude that South Africans strive to convey. There is a strong use of metaphor in *Sunrise Over South Africa,* comparing the odd-looking penguins, for example, to the late Charlie Chaplin.

The collection and the country of South Africa become a metaphor for collective hope and aspiration and a father's dream of a loving and kind world for his wife and children. Filled with stories of adventure, song, and dance, and the quiet moments in between, *Sunrise over South Africa* imbued me with a sense of magic, hopefulness, and renewed peace.

—Paul Zietsman, *Readers' Favorite* Five-Star Book Review of *Sunrise Over South Africa*

Sardines by the Gate

Airlines limbo,
international terminal,
packed like sardines
by the gate,
a gorgeous pile-up
of people waiting
to board flights
to either Dublin
or Amsterdam,
flight attendant crews in
sharp suits of
green and light blue
go by like military
marchers in a parade,
everyone wondering
what the hold-up is,
big flying people movers
that sometimes don't move
a millimeter or an inch
for all the tired human sardines
sipping soft drinks
and sighing, wanting so much
to soar to their destinations,
lovers, families and friends,
but stuck in silent stillness instead.

Eleven Languages

Without language, one cannot talk to people and understand them;
one cannot share their hopes and aspirations, grasp their history,
appreciate their poetry, or savor their songs.
—Nelson Mandela

I've heard that
eleven languages are
spoken in South Africa,
which seems
both a bit amazing
and frightening.
If all of those
languages were being
spoken in one room at the
same time,
how would anyone
understand anyone else;
would the United Nations
be needed to sort out the
lunch order
or settle a grimace or a gripe?
God would certainly look down
with a grin and laugh lightly and
lovingly in eleven languages
back at all of them on a
shining hungry early afternoon
heavenly sky-blue day.

The Big Bronze Bears

Four hours to while away between flights
at Amsterdam's sleek Schiphol airport,
walking slowly down
the colorful corridors
with bags wheeled behind,
taking in the bright signage
and modern, classy décor,
suddenly two huge
bronze bear sculptures appear
as if dropped into
sitting positions by
the same giant imaginary child
who built Stonehenge
out of chiseled craggy building blocks
during a morning's fun play,
the bears beckon,
and I sit on a set of massive legs
for a picture,
the two big shiny resting figures
are back-to-back,
waiting for the child in
every traveler's heart to appear.

So Many Screens

So many bright-lit screens
when it's dark at night
and people have awakened
from fitful bursts of sleep
on the plane over Africa,
a TV behind every seat
beaming a movie or show,
you look at your own movie
but inevitably glance at the screens
in the row ahead
or across the aisle and,
suddenly, when you stand up to stretch,
you're in a symphony of flickering
light and shadows,
surrounded, held captive
by a hundred beacons in the
wilderness of modern connectivity,
all of us escaping into worlds away
from the aches and pains of
a long twelve-hour Amsterdam
to Johannesburg flight.

The Hot Towel

The beauty of
the hot towel,
given out like
sweet gold to
surprised passengers
on an overseas flight,
is a throwback to
earlier days
when flying was
an elegant business,
a touch of humanity
in a hurly-burly
instantaneous "now" world,
handed softly with
a pair of long tongs,
the heat spreads through
your hands and
makes you smile,
thinking of your grandparents,
cut grass and hay,
summer visits to friends
by a cool lake,
Mom's chocolate chip brownies
coming from the oven
and Grandma's fabulous apple pie.

A Hamburger at Woolworths

First day in Johannesburg,
sleeping late to shake off
the slouching jet lag beast,
wandering down the
streets to an African Craft Market
full of stalls of carved
canes, wooden elephants and
handwoven baskets, as well as
colorful scarves,
drums and paintings
from all over this vast country,
each vendor welcoming you
to view his or her wares
with a friendly word
and a persistent manner.
Back up and outside for
a breath of fresh air,
we spotted a Woolworths
with a rustic café,
sat down at a long wooden table
and ordered tea, hot chocolate,
cokes, and some hamburgers while
watching the world and people go by,
thinking later that really good french fries
are a treasure a family can always share,
and that the few F.W. Woolworth department
stores of dim childhood memories—

fun "five-and-dime" places that had
shiny things and tasty candies for kids to buy
(and a small curved counter diner with a hot griddle
and worn swivel stools in the back)—
seem to have vanished without a trace
back home in the States,

but here in Johannesburg, something with
the same name (but owned by a different company)
has emerged in a modern, hip, and upscale way,
like a rare, thought-to-be-extinct animal emerging suddenly
from the jungles into the bright high sun
wearing a snappy tuxedo, a confident grin and pair of
beautifully polished leather dress shoes.

Nelson Mandela's Home

*Do not judge me by my successes, judge me by
how many times I fell down and got back up again.*
                                —Nelson Mandela

Plain red bricks,
small wood stove,
tiny white rooms,
one outside faucet,
proud old tree where the
family umbilical cords
were buried to stay
strong with history,
the humble,
simple
home
of one great man.

The African Drum

Rough carved beast,
coaxed out of the wood
with sharp tools, a good eye
and the will to create,
coated with purple dye,
swirls, circles and lines,
thin twisted black ropes
pulled down and holding tight
to taut white goat skin,
ready to be pounded
and carry the sound,
tap, slap, slither, snap,
you're part of the animal world,
making your own beat
as you slide through the jungle
of cars, buses, asphalt and cement,
up to your hotel room
to *rum-pum-pum-pum* away to
your heart's content in busy Jo'burg,
after the cool Sunday Craft
Market with hundreds of stalls
at the top of the tiered parking lot
closes slowly down like a child's eyes
just before the soft-shoe slip into happy
innocent, easy sleep.

The Soul of Soweto

For to be free is not merely to cast off one's chains, but to live in a way that respects and enhances the freedom of others.
—Nelson Mandela

The Soul of Soweto
is full of sadness,
sorry, and sighs,
but there is also
hope and light
beneath the little shacks
with corrugated steel
roofs held down by rocks,
there is desperation
but a will to live,
the schoolchildren
look neat in blue uniforms,
the laundry is hung
on lines in almost all yards,
but there is a constant inner cry
and flow of hidden tears in
the dust and debris
for the children who died
in the Soweto Uprising of 1976.

The Bright Light

I am the master of my fate; I am the Captain of my Soul.
                                        —Nelson Mandela

Nelson Mandela
was a man of many parts
and deep twenty-seven-years—
trapped-in-jail thoughts,
beloved by the people
and admired for his unshakable
convictions, he was
definitely the captain of
his soul and
the finest guide for steering
your own inner compass
in the proper
direction towards
the true, the right
and the bright glowing light.

Monkeys in the Fields

Monkeys in the fields,
pulling off oranges
from little bushes
to quietly feed,
before angry farmers
swoop in to
shoo them swiftly away.

The Potholes at Bourke's Luck

Red cliff walls,
jagged box of blocks,
canyons shaped
by waterfalls flowing
smoothly with a
soothing sound,
huge round potholes
punched through the rocks
as though by
a giant's gargantuan power drill,
beautiful vista views
from many rocky points
on the climbs up and down,
peaceful like a soft
quiet cello note or prayer.

Canyons on the Curves

Canyons around every curve,
mountains blue, round
and deep in the distance,
clouds and light touching
each surface with
a gentle afternoon hand.

A Formidable Combination

*A good head and a good heart
are always a formidable combination.*
—Nelson Mandela

When your thoughts
match your emotions
you're a prizefighter
of staggering depth
and magic moves in the ring,
able to dance to your
own inner music,
your soul pure
and unfiltered,
listening to bells rung
in other dimensions
like sweet clocks that
show the way but tell
no time,
a formidable combination,
a two-shot
to the solar plexus of the skies.

A Tower of Giraffes

Giraffes are
incredibly tall,
grazing like huge
construction cranes
in the treetops,
their necks
so impossibly long,
but there is an unexpected
grace to their movements
as they pace around
in twos and threes
in the wild,
their ears perk up
and they look across the field
and know you are there,
and what a beautiful
gallop when they run!

The Lioness

*Man's goodness is a flame that can be hidden,
but never extinguished.*
—Nelson Mandela

The lioness lies
long, regal, and still along
the edge of the dirt road,
watching the Kruger National Park
safari vehicles go by,
unfazed by loads
of picture-takers or
vehicles stopped at
strange angles around her
in a semicircle,
she's just enjoying the
early afternoon warmth
of the sun, but don't
be fooled by her coyness,
she could leap up anytime
quick as a cat and have you
for a tasty lunch!

The Hyena Pups

Brown hyena pups,
eight at least,
nursing at their
mother's underside
just beyond the Kruger Park road edge,
surrounded by slightly
older brothers and sisters moving about,
a scene of domestic bliss
in a tough-as-nails
wildlife habitat,
a pup climbs over
her side
and hangs there,
new to the world
and feeling the way to grow
under Mom's watchful,
loving eye.

A Dazzle of Zebras

A dazzle of zebras
was gathered next to the
Kruger Park road, just
a few yards from
our vehicle, their
stripes so hard to believe;
how could such an animal
exist and, yet, there they are
in the wild, adults and
young ones, interacting,
feeding, grazing, growing.

Wind Whipping Through the Safari Jeep

Wind whipping through the
safari jeep; open on all sides,
hair flying in all directions,
sudden angular stop
to view water buffalo
huddled in a large bunch
called an "obstinacy"
at Kruger National Park,
the beige winter savanna stretching
everywhere for hundreds of miles,
the buffalo horns curling
up like Salvador Dali's mustache,
dark black, formidable,
looking at us with relaxed
but sinister eyes,
big bodies lying down and partially
hidden in tall grass,
daring someone to approach
and test their mettle.

Giraffes on the Run

*One cannot be prepared for something while secretly
believing it will not happen.*
—Nelson Mandela

Giraffes on the run,
loping across the road,
two impossibly long necks
with beautiful brown and beige spots,
graceful and surprisingly fast,
turning back to look
at the people in safe safari jeeps
holding their collective breaths
and quietly snapping shots,
so tall and yet so agile,
as if emerging from
an enchanted winter's
savanna dream to eat
and commune with
the curved green
Acacia treetops.

The Bathroom Attendant

A nation should not be judged by how it treats its highest citizens, but its lowest ones.
—Nelson Mandela

The bathroom attendant
was washing down the
sinks and mopping the
floors in the Ezulwini Valley hotel,
paying attention to
the smallest detail,
a hairnet on his head,
plastic gloves on his hands,
I thanked him for
the fine job he was doing
and he proudly said,
"This is my office."

Sunrise Over South Africa

African sunrise,
glowing red ball
peeking out from
behind a mountain,
white mist filling the
lowest areas of land,
little boys dressed in
blue sweaters and slacks
for school waving
and getting into
a small van,
while the red ball
rises and takes over
the sky.

Two Poachers

So many rhinos
shot by poachers
sneaking into Kruger National
Park with sophisticated equipment,
the rhino's horn worth
hundreds of thousands
in China, where it's
crushed and mixed into
mysterious aphrodisiac potions,
but last night the park guards
shot two poachers in order
to protect the mighty rugged beasts,
the hunters suddenly
became the hunted,
but will now hunt and
hurt no more,
until the next set of
swift and silent
nighttime poachers
comes slithering and soft-shoeing along.

The Macadamia Nut Man

We must use time creatively, and forever realize that the time is always ripe to do right.
—Nelson Mandela

The man named Jason selling
macadamia nuts
met the bus in Dullstroom
and showed his wares,
three kinds, all
neatly wrapped,
but then he offered
a taste and I fell
hook, line, and sinker
for the roasted buttery sweet
ones, so good
and soul-soothing I almost
summersaulted in
the Mpumalanga Province.

Harrie's Pancakes

We stop
for beautiful
rolled-up pancakes
with any filling
you can think of
—even Thai food—
and brown sugar
& cinnamon
and then continue
on over bumpy roads
through contoured
landscapes full of
cattle, little lakes,
scenic hills in the distance
and dark black mounds
of harvested coal,
the lonely single
trees on the rolling mountains
calling out like African songs.

South Africanisms

Jam=Jelly
Jelly=Jello
Loo=Bathroom
Brilliant=Great
Collect=Pickup Area
KFC=Chicken Shops Everywhere
Still=Regular Bottled Water
Sparkling=Bubbly Bottled Water
Coach=Luxury Bus
Bum=Rear End
Pavement=Sidewalk
To Let= For Rent
Petrol=Fuel
Sorted Out=Figured Out
Geyser=Water Tank
Slap Chips=Deep Fried Potatoes
Skinner=Gossip
Lekker=Great, Nice, Tasty
Kief=Cool
Howzit=How's it Going?
Yebo=Yes
Braai=Barbecue
Cozzie=Swimsuit
Sharp Sharp=Goodbye
Lulu=Laugh
Robot=Traffic Light
Tekkies, Takkies=Sneakers
Doss=Sleep
Mooing=To Flirt
Jol=To Have Fun

Hayibo=Wow
Larny=Something Fancy
Whatookal=Whatever
Krimpie=Old Person
Aikona=Not on Your Life
Eish=Surprise, or Hurt, or Exasperation
Just Now=A Bit Later
Ag, Man=Oh Man!
Yoh!=You Scared Me
Izzit=Is it?
Vry=Kiss
Dof=Stupid
Eina=Ouch
Voetsek=Go Away
Mal=Crazy

Zulu Wedding Dance

The drums pounding out
a rhythmic Zulu tribal beat,
bum, bum, bum, bum,
bum, bum, bum, bum,
Zulu women in colorful garments
singing, with many unusual
high-pitched notes,
the Zulu warrior men
dancing against one
another, each competing
for the highest leg kicks
and creative moves,
while one leader shouts
out encouragement
and runs back and forth,
an amazing display
of culture and history
on the sand in a Zulu
village surrounded by a
thick fence made of
beautiful wild-shaped branches.

A Piece of Chocolate

There is nothing like returning to a place that remains unchanged to find the ways in which you yourself have altered.
—Nelson Mandela

On the road to Eswatini
a tiny country with
a king within South Africa
and a bag of Ghirardelli
chocolates is passed around
the bus, the taste of
caramel and dark chocolate
a treat for the tongue and soul
while mountains covered in
light fog sit in the distance,
a sleepy road crew waves
us on with an orange flag,
cattle stand by a passing fence
looking bored, as if unable
to find a poker game,
and ten women wrapped
in colorful blankets in the open back
space of a pickup truck (their heads
swirled in black and white scarves)

wave and smile and play hide and seek,
covering and uncovering their eyes
with unexpected early morning joy
and fun as the pickup truck rumbles
ahead before pulling into a gas
station while we zip on hurriedly by.

Woman Under a Curved Tree

Live life as though nobody is watching, and express yourself as though everyone is listening.
—Nelson Mandela

Woman under a curved tree
just past the Eswatini border
sitting on a wooden bench,
her long red plastic bags of
oranges hanging
from the roof edge of a
small roadside store shed,
waiting for a customer
to come by.

The Glassblowers of Eswatini

Bright hot glass
pulled from big dull
steel boxes
like little suns
from the center
of the earth,
long metal poles
coming and going
across the factory floor
in smooth rhythm,
orange jumpsuits
everywhere,
—a furious hubbub of activity—
the shapers shape,
the polishers polish,
the carriers carry,
in a sizzling oven of a room
for turning wheelbarrows of recycled glass
into fine finished products
for gleaming store shelves
next door, nearby and far away.

The Operatic Dinner Singer

Where you stand depends on where you sit.
—Nelson Mandela

In the middle of a hotel
buffet dinner,
an operatic voice is heard
singing "Happy Birthday"
with professional gusto
at a table nearby,
and then this happens
again and again as if
everyone at the hotel
or restaurant is somehow
simultaneously experiencing
a birthday celebration tonight,
but the singer is great,
a young Plácido Domingo
in the making, dressed
in a smart suit jacket and cravat,
belting out those glorious
low notes and transforming
the simple song into a work
of joy-filled bravura vocal art.

Two Lane Road

Two lane road,
faded asphalt
and faint white stripes
down the middle
like Morse code,
dot dash dot dot,
calling to the corn
and grass and trees
with a soft whisper
of sweet promises
and things unseen,
the billboards
and green-blue signs
funneling you home
like a sideways tornado
of constantly spinning time.

I Blew the Fuse

Tread softly, breathe peacefully, laugh hysterically.
—Nelson Mandela

I blew the fuse
in the Eswatini hotel room.
I was pulling an open suitcase
strap on a table and it
released too fast
and I knocked over
a lamp and then
when I tried to put
the lamp parts back
together, there was a sudden
spark and explosion
and the lamp blew, the
wall socket sparked
and the room went black.
Luckily it was morning and
there was daylight
streaming all around,
but I checked our sons'
room two doors down and all of the
electricity was out there, too.
Suddenly, I noticed that a large swath of
the hallway lights were completely out
and then a blond-haired lady emerged
from her room holding her curling iron

and said the lights
in her room were out and she couldn't
finish doing her hair.
She asked if my room was out, too,
and I stumblingly answered, "yes, same thing for us."
It was beyond belief: I had taken out
an entire hotel hallway and
at least six rooms with my
lamp-wrestling episode.
I put the lamp back the way it was,
and made a hurried search for fuse panels,
but the only ones I found were locked.
My wife and I then slowly closed our door and
tiptoed softly to the elevators with our sons
and suitcases in order to make our way down
to the tour bus since it was checkout day.
It was like something out of a *Laurel & Hardy* or
Three Stooges comedy movie and I slunk out of Eswatini
in disbelief with my head down, but my wife and I
were also quietly giggling at the surreal craziness of it all.
Just to play it safe, I notified the front desk
about the room and hallway lights
going out so that someone could check
on this and quickly reset or replace the fuses.

I told the desk clerk something weird must have
happened up there (and to be sure, it did!).
The whole thing reminded me of a pillow fight
I had with my older brother in a Prague
hotel room in 1968 when we were little kids on
our first European trip with our parents
right before the Soviet tanks rolled into Czechoslovakia.
That time, a hotel lamp broke due to an errant pillow throw
and we hid the lamp in the closet under a blanket
so that we wouldn't be arrested and thrown in jail.
Our tour high-tailed it out of that country
ahead of the troop invasion to quell the
country's liberalization reforms and protests,
but somehow, I was sure the broken
hotel room lamp was responsible for the conflict.
There must be some convoluted
cosmic forces at work
in my life to make these
mysterious lamp-related situations
take place in foreign countries.
At least that's what I think happened
in Eswatini when I opened my
suitcase, pulled the strap, hit the lamp
and blew the bloody fuse.

Braai

South Africans
love grilled meats
(called "braai"),
chicken,
roast beef,
sausages
and more,
all sizzling and neat,
the amazing smells pulling you close,
but the word is (from one of our safari guides)
that warthog is a surprisingly
tasty treat (and very tender, too),
but watch out for water buffalo meat,
since it's as rough and tough
and tumble as the unpredictable
thick-hided animal itself,
(which can fiercely charge at any time
and fights with a fury that
knows no bounds).

Searching for Hippos

Gliding on the
St. Lucia Estuary
within the iSimangaliso Wetland
Park World Heritage Site,
looking for hippos
and there they are,
floating on one side
of the boat
or trying to keep up
with us on the other side,
just a head, eyes and a bit
of body showing,
but later we see ten
hippos resting on a muddy
riverbank, their bodies
fully exposed and they're
huge, like massive grey
stones, just amazingly
large round creatures
taking a break and lying in
the sun together
as one,
happy to be near each other
with waving grasses green & tall
all around.

Elephants and Dirt

Lead from the back—and let others believe they are in front.
—Nelson Mandela

Elephants standing
in a big bush
in Hluhluwe-iMfolozi Park,
tossing dirt
up and over their
backs with flexible long grey
snouts,
splashing the red dirt
and dust all over
their bodies to keep
bugs away,
could they tell we
were watching them
from the nearby hill?

Feet to the Fire

Shoes up against the
rim of the huge metal
fire pit at the
simple rustic lodge in
Hluhluwe-iMfolozi Park,
nighttime has fallen
like a gentle blanket
and all are in bed
in the thatched roof
circular cottages but
the two of us
sipping glasses of
soft soothing wine
and gazing at the
oranges and reds of
the burning logs,
listening to the
bird and animal
sounds of the
South African
night all around.

The Gurgling Drain

The gurgling shower
drain with its
glug-glug-glug-glug sounds
made us think of
birds in the outside trees
or busy baboons on the grounds.

The Peace of the Rolling Road

The coach rolls on,
lulling eyes to sleep
despite the endless
beauty of curved contoured ground
and ever-changing landscapes,
a rhythmic peace
descends and blesses
with the soft and
caressing song of
the moving mellifluous open road.

The Mountains of South Africa

I never lose. I either win or learn.
—Nelson Mandela

The mountains of South Africa
seem to be always there,
like a good, trusted friend
in the distance,
surrounding you with
love, grand views and quiet strength
to give you peaceful thoughts in your
wide, world-traveling dreams.

Baboons on the Road

Black baboons on the
curving mountain road
scattering before the
slowing bus,
scampering four-legged
towards, under, and over
the guard-rail,
looking back frightenedly
at the behemoth of rubber
and steel bearing down,
a last lone baboon
brother or sister left
on the other side
of the road until
the great wheeled whale of
people passes by.

Swimming in South Africa

The alluring outdoor pool
at our Gqeberha hotel
was so shockingly cold I believe
that fully-bundled Alaskan Artic
Circle Inuit Natives could freeze
their winter-toughened toes.
It looked so inviting, so lovely
and so empty of swimmers
and I wanted to try my hand
at swimming once in South Africa,
even though the sun was going down
on the horizon and the temperatures
were starting to dip.
It seemed like a good idea at the time,
so I changed into my swimsuit
and dove in, thinking things would be
a breeze, but as I hit the water,
I realized that what I was actually
involved in was more like
a sub-zero polar lake-plunge in mid-winter.
The cold engulfed me like an iceberg with mighty arms,
dragging me down and punching all
of the oxygen out of my body.
It was a bit surreal to be under the
water and thinking I had been flash
frozen like a bag of Birds Eye peas and
all I really wanted was to rewind the film and
stop back at the pool edge before I dove in.
Transformed into a big flailing human popsicle,

I began to claw my way back up to the top
and broke through the water, sucking in
air furiously as though I had never breathed
something so sweet and deep before.

I smiled and waved to my family
standing nearby around the pool edge
and swam as fast as I could to the ladder
and climbed out, shaking like a leaf,
happy to say I had given it a go, but
wondering now why I had been lunatic enough
to try, but sometimes as a Dad you just
decide to do goofy, fun stuff in order
to cut loose and it was kind of cool in my mind
to say that I had survived a swim in a
crazy-cold unheated outdoor wintertime
South African pool (with "cool" definitely
being the operative memorable mumbled word).

Touching the Waters

Touching the warm
Indian Ocean,
the waves dancing
over the beach
like the ticks of a clock,
seashells scattered in
a five-foot-long layer
as far as the eye can
see,
hundreds of black birds
sitting in the water in
a circle,
a hint of dolphins
jumping somewhere,
the cloudy sky just letting
in small cries of light,
the holiness of the short moment
worn quietly like
the weight of a key in the
secret lock of the Universe
in the palm of your ocean-wet hand.

Dance Party at the Durban Airport

*What counts in life is not the mere fact that we have lived.
It is what difference we have made to the lives of others
that will determine the significance of the life we lead.*
—Nelson Mandela

The singing at the
Durban airport
started slowly
and grew louder and
louder until it
attracted people from
all around,
the singers stood in a ring,
swaying in a rhythmic dance
and clapping their hands
while chanting a hypnotic
song with back-and-forth responses,
the smiles spread and soon other rings
of people were around
the singers singing along,
before a big dance party broke out and
took over the airport lobby,
something to hear & see
and join in on,
I think it might have been
a school sports team
heading to a national competition,
the whole thing kind of amazing,

grabbing your heart & soul
just like the cheering
chanting group
dressed in shiny blue track suits did
at the gas station/market
rest stop on the way to the airport,
such joy and happiness
unfettered, unlimited and manifold.

Indian Ocean Sun

Bright sun bouncing off the
Indian Ocean,
endless ripples through the water
seen from a South African
Airways flight window
overhead,
freighters and other ships pass
by in a wink,
to be like a bird is
an amazing thing,
something daVinci could only sketch
and dream about years ago,
light as a feather
soaring towards land
and sand, each place
a temporary but welcome home.

The Waves and the Mouth

The "mouth" of Tsitsikamma
National Park is spectacular,
waves crashing over jagged
streaked rocks, steep wooden
staircases, winding paths
through overgrown vegetation,
craggy trees and vines,
up down up down
round and round,
little white rope
your only hope,
scoot and slide
down the hillside
to a dazzling suspension bridge
with a wooden floor
and four young tourists
bouncing up and down
to sway the bridge from side-to-side
just as you reach the middle
(which widens your eyes and
makes you grab the steel rails for support
while whispering a silent prayer),
but you survive and
happily
make it,
intact, to the other equally-dramatic side.

The Knysna Fires

*The brave man is not he who does not feel afraid,
but he who conquers that fear.*
                              —Nelson Mandela

The 2017 Knysna fires
must have been
horrible to experience
firsthand,
destroying the Featherbed
Nature Reserve and many forests
and homes,
seven lost their lives,
and you can see the hills blackened
with twisted burned
gnarled trees, plants
and bushes,
some scorched houses are caved-in
but others nearby have
miraculously survived,
the bad drought
and strong winds spread
the fire all over,
flaming pine cones
became ghastly grenades when blown about,

but the town of Knysna survived,
on a beautiful estuary,
now peaceful and still,
a shrine to the torched dark aftermath all around,
but there is some green left in places on the
devastated hills;
life begins again, the
resilience of people, plants and trees
a remarkable hungry thing.

The Knysna Seahorse

The Knysna seahorse
is very rare
and hard to see
(are you really there?)

In a tiny tank,
at a tiny nature place,
beige, shy, and hiding,
a mini seahorse face.

Such a strange
and marvelous sight,
morning, noon,
and late at night.

A type of horse
you just can't ride,
but, boy-oh-boy, does it have
the will to survive.

Talking to My Sons

May your choices reflect your hopes, not your fears.
                            —Nelson Mandela

Talking to my sons
over pizza in Knysna,
thin crust, wood fired & oven-baked,
tasty, hot, and
well-crafted by people
who know how a pizza should be made,
my lovely wife watching
us happily, dividing
up the salad that arrives,
a dreamy traveler's
look in her eye,
all of us laughing at
good and bad jokes and the
puns we were making
up on the spot like jazz musicians riffing
on each other's ideas,
a happy joshing jesting bunch,
a dazzle of a family enjoying
the wonderful loud textured din
of love, togetherness, pizza and life.

The Shantytowns

There can be no greater gift than that of giving one's time and energy to helping others without expecting anything in return.
—Nelson Mandela

Outside each larger city
in South Africa
there are shantytowns
made of simple corrugated
steel roofs and sides,
with cloths hanging down
over windows,
shack after small
homemade shack
crammed into tiny
spaces, all filled
with workers looking
for jobs (*any* job
in the city), happy
to take lowly service positions
and do the work well for the tips
that can hopefully get them
out of the shacks and into
government-built housing
with red roofs, colorful walls,
two bedrooms and a solar-heated
sideways round barrel water tank
on the roof called a geyser.

Cars on the Wrong Side of the Road

Seeing cars on the wrong side of
the road takes a while to get used to,
you always feel like
the bus is turning into
traffic, but it all works out,
however, walking across
3- or 4-way intersections
is a bit of a roll of the dice
and you have to think fast to
decide who is turning which
way into the when and where,
but if you follow
the locals as they
walk, you'll be just fine
(most of the time).

Wind Turbines Turning Slowly

Wind turbines
turning slowly,
tall white towers
looming over the
landscape in herds
here and there
on the way to Cape Town,
a new modern animal
competing with the
giraffes for the
hard-to-get height award.
A group of giraffes in
motion is called
a "journey,"
but these new white
metal tower animals just
stand still, never moving any legs,
staring all down with the eyes
of the future, and the need of the now.

Cleopatra's Needle

Into the Cango Caves
high in the mountains,
the temperature doesn't
drop, the dankness
of normal caves doesn't
chill, which is a bit
baffling, but a mountain
cave is different than
one deep in the earth,
more humid and tolerable,
here full of spectacular
stalagmites and stalactites
from ceilings and floors,
some meeting in the middle
to form columns like *Cleopatra's
Needle,* which may be
150,000 years old.
The dreadlocked,
theatrically-voiced guide
takes us from room to room
to describe the darkened sights
with a flashlight, before illuminating
everything with well-placed uplights,
the ceilings and walls as beautiful as
those in the Sistine Chapel,
making us spin in slow circles to
take in all the glorious shapes,

stunned at the magnificence that nature
can slowly create in dark silence until
someone comes along to pull such
strange quiet wild things
into the sound and the light.

The Ostriches of Oudtshoorn

So many ostriches
coming at you,
with long fluid necks
and big beaks,
and faster strides than
you ever thought possible,
each one looking at
you curiously with
those clever ostrich eyes.
Up to four hundred pounds,
with a dangerous claw nail,
but inquisitive and friendly, too
(just look out for your glasses and
watch or they'll soon be snatched
and snarfed away for a midday snack!),
they took feed pellets from my hand,
but then the beaks closed hard on
my fingers and I pulled away with a jump,
later touching one big bird's feathers,
light as a passing cloud.

The Aloe Tree

There it was,
the world's biggest
aloe tree statue
across from the aloe
products factory,
it looked so real
surrounded by little
live aloe trees
(spiky with tall red-stem flowers)
that I had to see it up close,
the craftmanship was
amazing down to the last detail,
it cast a long aloe shadow
and I tipped an imaginary cap
in its direction to the
dreamlike quality of
this fleeting, surreal pause
in travel time.

The Soup in Swellendam

*I like friends who have independent minds because
they tend to make you see problems from all angles.*
—Nelson Mandela

The soup in Swellendam
was so good it floated
up off the spoon,
a marvelous mixture of
lentils and vegetables
spun into a fine broth,
it glided, glistened
and glowed
and put a fine light
in all of us gathered
like apostles around
the large communal
lunchtime table.

Rugby, Cricket, Soccer

Know your enemy—and learn about his favorite sport.
—Nelson Mandela

Rugby,
cricket,
soccer,
rugby,
soccer,
cricket,
bike racing,
cricket (plus some soccer),
sometimes some
news or a movie
slipped in between the cracks,
the hotel TV channels
limited but full of
sports at all times,
day or night,
and a good thing
it is, too,
for a country must
have its heroes and competitions
to pull men and women
together
and distract them
from the sameness
of daily life between
the moon, sun and stars.

The Average South African Has Never Seen Snow

When the water starts boiling it is foolish to turn off the heat.
—Nelson Mandela

Besides brief sightings
in the mountains from a distance,
the average South African
has never seen snow,
due to the moderate
temperatures and warmer
climate all year round.
Our tour guide,
a Capetonian
(originally from Durban),
once went to Montreal
and finally saw white flakes
falling and jumped up
from the restaurant
dinner table
to race out into the
street and see the snow.
What a magical moment,
surrounded by a gentle cotton cloud in the cold,
seeing something never seen before,
white fluttering diamonds
coming down from the sky.

Head in the Clouds

*After climbing a great hill, one only finds
that there are many more hills to climb.*
—Nelson Mandela

Top of the mountain,
reaching out to touch
the clouds
so close they could
be in your pocket,
so cold up high,
the view down to
Cape Town below
showing tiny wonders,
little buildings and cars,
like a child's set of toys,
the sun shining clean
and bright,
the rocks full of puddles,
the curving paths
pulling voyagers on
twists and turns for
pictures or quiet
moments of contemplation,
the mug of hot tea in the café
offering welcome warmth
as the sun dances down the cliffs
to the rippling ocean below.

The Tree Canopy Walk in the Garden

The beautiful wooden
snake of a treetop canopy walk
at the Kirstenbosch National Botanic Garden
is a dizzying dazzle
of dark brown curving
wood with sinuous metal
sides that look like
nets thrown out by simple fishermen
to catch curious humans
swimming through the
lush green foliages on all sides,
but the views from this
sensuous serpentine path
of the mountains are
heart-stopping and
then you feel the walkway
swaying under your feet
like a tree bending in a breeze.

The Company's Garden

Strolling in The Company's
Garden in Cape Town
on a rainy morning,
just the four of us
and a few wet
passersby,
the canopy of trees
covering us with
an umbrella of leaves
and branches,
the controversial Cecil Rhodes
statue straight ahead,
a café swing with
a huge climb-in basket
suspended on long sturdy ropes
appears to the right,
catches our easy-going
eyes, and makes
us laugh in sweet
smiling surprise.

The Africa Café

Huge forbidding door
opens and gives way
to a high-ceilinged
hall with a burst
of colors (gold, yellow, black, red),
women dressed in bright salmon,
chartreuse, turquoise and gold caftans
with tilted hats
and long multiple necklaces—
their faces painted with dots and dashes—
seat you in a breathtaking room
full of African-artist-painted
walls decorated in a delightful, fun way,
the light fixtures
made of crazy red wire floating in all
directions like birds,
the menu written on the inside
of an inner-lit glass jar
but there is no choice
to be made, the food just comes out
in little bowls that are later replaced with
other little bowls and all are sublime,
the waiters and waitresses then start singing
African chant-like songs while pounding
a big drum held by in the air by one man
(the women thump the drum the hardest with both hands),
the air filled with energy, clapping and laughter,
you are transported to another dimension
and soaring free like an eagle in the clear blue sky.

The Man in the Van

It always seems impossible, until it's done.
—Nelson Mandela

The man in the van
was elegant,
blue tie,
neat suit
a quiet-spoken gentleman
who spoke of Apartheid
and how his entire family
was thrown out of his home
as a child and moved out to
a faraway portion of Cape Town.
Even worse, his brother
was shot and killed during the
1976 Soweto Uprising and
he himself took a bullet in the leg.
The search for his brother's
body took weeks until
they found him buried at
the bottom of a horrendous human pile,

and the family never really found out what
had actually happened to him.
The driver was so soft-spoken we had to lean up close
from the back seats to hear him,
this dapper dignified man who had seen it all up close
and felt the fury of the fight for democracy
and a new way of life.

The Good Driver

*It is not where you start but how high you aim
that matters for success.*
—Nelson Mandela

Adanam,
the good taxi driver in Cape Town
guiding us to
an almost unfindable
dinner place
hidden away in a building,
cheerfully describing his
hometown,
happy about his wife and
first child on the way,
skillfully navigating
the hectic left-side-of-the-road traffic,
the restaurant is hip with
no menu (just steak, salad & fries
for everyone) and cool, sleek people
dressed in black, the pounding
bass beat music bringing a strange
excitement into the room with
fanciful white hanging lampshades
and the chefs visible, grilling up the meals.
Afterwards, Adanam
returns and takes us to Marco's for
terrific African music, the 3-marimba,
1-drummer, 2-female-singer band

hot, swooping & pulsing, and one of the singers
is fantastic, like a young Mavis Staples,
diving into each African song as if it's in her blood
and the crowd sings back at her in the call &
response choruses,
a night of unplanned, fortunate free-wheeling magic
due to our friend and guide,
the good driver, Adanam.

A Round at the Royal Cape Golf Club

Racing in a taxi
from the bottom of
Table Mountain to
the Royal Cape Golf Club course
(the oldest one in Africa,
dating back to 1885),
the cab driver speaks
of Nelson Mandela
and a tear runs down
his cheek and we talk
about the current government
problems, the city, crime,
and the shantytowns,
eventually, we arrive, and
I disembark and race in
to grab some rental sticks and a pull
trolley to make my tee time
with a minute to spare, but
then the starter notices my jeans and says
there's a dress code and scrambles to find me
a pair of rain pants to put over my jeans,
and the crisis is resolved, so I
play the round in two pairs of pants,
walking alone in the sun, Table Mountain
in the distance like a joyful, hopeful
presence guiding us all along,
thinking about the cab driver and his
moving memories and tears.

Golf in the Sunshine

There is no passion to be found playing small—
in settling for a life that is less than the one
you are capable of living.
      —Nelson Mandela

Walking alone
in the South African sun,
hearing the hoot of an owl,
the honk of a goose (cormorant?)
and the light *knock-knock-knock*
sound of tiny frogs in the
drought-lowered ponds
and lakes,
in the zone and swinging true and free,
deep in quiet thoughts,
thanking God from time
to time for my family,
the beauty of the mountains and the day
and the way life zig-zags
in the direction it wants you to go,
jump on board and ride the train
to destinations unknown
and find the deep love of a life full of
ups and downs, peaks and valleys and
soft soaring moments of
glorious light and endless wonder.

The Stone Masons

Everyone can rise above their circumstances and achieve success if they are dedicated to and passionate about what they do.
—Nelson Mandela

The stone masons
sat in a pile of rocks
under some trees
to the side of a golf hole,
chipping away on
large rocks with
hammers and chisels to
shape the stone
into pieces for the
mysterious boxes by the
Royal Cape Golf Club course
tee areas for each hole,
rectangular two-level shapes
full of sand with
beautiful earth-toned stone
expertly laid and cemented,
but the stone masons
made a mesmerizing sound,
banging away as I went past,

the hammer blows coming
one after another in
a beautiful rhythm
like the ticks of a
celestial clock counting
off the time
and heralding the future of
the world's fate,
sculpted one carefully
crafted & chiseled stone at a time.

Dinner in a South African Home

*Education is the most powerful weapon
which you can use to change the world.*
—Nelson Mandela

The big table for fifteen
was set in a South African
husband and wife's home,
the couple kind enough
to open their doors
to the conversations and questions
of eager-eyed travelers,
another local longtime
friend joined us, too,
and it was like we had
all known each other for years;
we spoke of home, weather,
travels, Cape Town, our dogs
and children and the interests of
my two teenaged sons,
we learned first-hand about Apartheid

and how few educational and job chances
there were for this elegant cheerful couple
who had nonetheless made it to
universities and careers despite
all of the obstacles and problems,
the hope lies with the new generation
who never experienced Apartheid
in all its evil hydra-headed horribleness,
and who carry their parents' hard work
and progress forward full of bright eyes
and boundless energy now.

Cable Car to Table Mountain

Clear day
after three cloudy ones,
we all run to Table Mountain
in droves
by taxi, foot, and bus
to take the wondrous
rotating cable car
up to the top
to view the city, harbor,
and surrounding mountains
in incredible ways.
Crisp, icy in places
and thrilling,
the top is generally level (like a table)
but full of craggy rocks
and walking paths
with outlooks for poses and photo snaps,
the sunlight shining on all faces,
God giving each and every one
there a special moment to commune
with nature and feast on the beauty
of a high gorgeous place
that's remote and inaccessible
on so many days, but today
it glows and stuns and the
world is soft, whole and
made of good hopeful things.

So Many Casks

So many casks
holding wine in a huge
temperature-controlled
vineyard warehouse
near the town of Stellenbosch
(in the countryside just
outside Cape Town),
row after row
stacked three or four shelves high
as far as the eye can see,
metal rims tucked in tight around
the oak pieces,
the wooden stave curves commingling
and adding flavor to the wine,
all from grapes picked mostly
by hand,
but the casks also conjure up
pirates, ships on the bounding main
and sailors passing the
Cape of Good Hope
in search of brilliant new
trade routes and rugged, swashbuckling
adventures yet to come.

The Southwesternmost Point of the African Continent

Cape of Good Hope,
so far south
only Antarctica is
next beyond the crashing waves,
tight "V" formations of flying birds,
swaying black fields of shallow
water kelp and
craggy beige and brown rocks,
wind whipping our faces
and hair, amazing vistas,
and an eland, the
largest of antelopes,
suddenly pops into view
before sauntering off into
the bushes, but the small flock
of ostriches rooting about in the soil nearby
is an added delight by the Atlantic,
which relentlessly pounds the rocks with
constant curling waves.

The Cape Point Lighthouse

Funicular train car to the
lighthouse at the
top of Cape Point,
misty wisps of fog
rolling in, shrouding
the hill and steps
and just starting
to cover the top of
the lighthouse peak,
the Atlantic and beach
visible on one side
but just white
fast-moving fog
coming up the cliffs
on the other,
as if a giant was blowing
hard from below,
magical and mysterious,
romantic in a black-and-white
Humphrey Bogart-Lauren Bacall
old movie way, looking at
all of the names and dates
written on the rocks,
at the top, holding hands
with the one you love.

The Flying Dutchman

The swift and silent funicular
train car took us up to
at the top of Cape Point
and a mysterious fog rolled
in, enshrouding the lighthouse
and making it impossible to see
anything on one side of the mountain,
it was a wild rolling, roiling,
upward-climbing white mist
that almost seemed as if it had
been shipped over to South Africa
from a Hollywood special effects
department to set the mood for a
1930s *Hound of the Baskervilles* movie
scene on a gloomy Dartmoor landscape
with Basil Rathbone puffing a pipe as Sherlock Holmes,
and then, there it was, a sign at the top
telling the story of the crazed ship captain
working for the Dutch East India Company

who tried to sail around the Cape of Good Hope
in a terrible storm and let loose a fateful curse
as his ship sank, which condemned the vessel and crew to sail
those waters until Doomsday,
a ghostly apparition that appears from time to time
in the mist and fog and scares all sailors
down to their boots and bones,
worried that the fearsome Flying Dutchman will take them
along for a deadly ride to Davy Jones's
sea-bottom locker in a horrible hurry, too.

The African Penguins at Boulders Beach

The African penguins
at Boulders Beach
are such funny
waddlers, many
walking like Charlie Chaplin
over the low sand dunes
to meet up with
their family members
or go for a refreshing
swim in the ocean,
diving through waves
as if they were nothing,
changing from weaving wobblers
into brilliant swimming machines
instantaneously,
only to return back to the beach
to hobnob and play with
sisters and brothers,
moms and dads,
and good old penguin friends,
many of whom are nesting
in dugout holes on twigs and branches
in order to lay eggs and create
the next generation,
so many nests and nesting holes
it seems to be a maternity ward,
with the newest arrivals all
brown and befuddled
and just figuring things out.

Puffs of Smoke

A winner is a dreamer who never gives up.
—Nelson Mandela

Who are we but
puffs of smoke
from the gentle pipe of an old man
sitting at the Cape of Good Hope
on the southwest tip of the African continent
watching the nearby penguins nest and play
in his ever-expanding mind,
a dreamer thinking of things
and places far away,
mulling the idea of unfurling
life upon the land
and watching it grow by leaps
and bounds,
rolling good and evil down the slope
together to see how the raucous wrestling
match turns out,
smiling at what will be and where the
journey might lead,
he longs for company,
for laughter and joy in the long dark night,
and welcomes the sun he's just made with
open arms and a full heart of sparkling diamonds each day.

Traveling with My Sons

*It is in your hands, to make a better world
for all who live in it.*
—Nelson Mandela

Traveling with my sons,
showing them the world
and other cultures,
languages, customs
and foods,
so that they know what's
out there away from
home,
what's different in other
countries and
what's the same,
how tough people have it
and yet how they smile
through the pain,
how clean and neat boys and girls look
when they emerge from
their corrugated metal shanty shacks
with hanging sheets and blankets
for windows, dressed in colorful
and well-pressed uniforms, heading
off to school to learn with a gleam
and playfulness in their eyes
as they laugh and wave to buses and cars passing by,

how lucky we are to
have two sons whose
eyes have been opened a little to the world,
perhaps they've each become a richer, deeper person,
someone who wants to change things,
to help, to give back in some way,
it's hard to say,
but I think seeing South Africa
changes you in a way that makes
you think and wonder
and grow, with deep roots like the
Acacia trees on the savanna,
gracefully arched and ready to shelter
whoever comes by, up and under
the far-reaching branches, to lean
for a quiet, thoughtful moment
against the strong sturdy steady trunk.

The Beauty of the Far, Far Away

Is there anything
better than doing
nothing with your
family in a foreign city
for a few hours before
or after touring,
TV on, a decent
movie to watch,
some snacks and waters
nearby,
stopping the world
and the fast-turning pace
for just a short while,
the mind relaxes
and you siesta without
a plan, you daydream
and drift, unconnected and
free like pieces of paper
blowing around in
friendly breezes,
the demands of home,
work, and the day
far, far away.

A Diamond in the Sun

*If there are dreams about a beautiful South Africa,
there are also roads that lead to their goal.
Two of these roads could be named Goodness and Forgiveness.*
                                   —Nelson Mandela

It felt a bit like we were in a
James Bond movie in South Africa,
changing locations so often,
seeing so many amazing and
dramatic types of landscapes—
mountains,
savannas,
oceans,
plateaus,
forests,
cliffs,
caves,
estuaries,
deserts,
grasslands—
the whole country so
overwhelming
in its rumbling massive
size, so full of so many moving,
magical sights,
you felt like you were on
a secret mission for a
cloak-and-dagger intelligence service
to observe and report back
in a quiet, clandestine way
what had been seen and felt

and experienced,
but how can you sum up
such a vast place where penguins, giraffes,
lions and elephants roam and the people moved
your heart with their long struggle for freedom
and the right to live their lives as
they choose,
what an incredibly bright and beautiful
diamond glistening in the sun,
which rises over this unforgettable country
each morning to touch each outstretched hand
and reach into your traveler's soul to
put a powerful seed of knowledge, understanding
and wisdom there in the hope that you'll
step on a plane and come back to embrace
this wondrous sprawling special place
sometime in the not-so-distant future again.

Sometimes, it falls upon a generation to be great.
You can be that great generation.
Let your greatness blossom.

—Nelson Mandela

About the Author

Joseph Kuhn Carey's previous full-length travel poetry collections, *Black Forest Dreams, A Journey Through Germany* (Kelsay Books, 2021) and *Postcards From Poland* (Chicago Poetry Press, 2014), have garnered numerous awards. His poetry has been nominated for a Pushcart Prize, selected in local and national contests, shown on buses and in store windows & parks, and published in many poetry collections, as well as in his chapbook, *Bulk-Rate* (The Reflex Press, 1981).

Joe received an American Society of Composers, Authors & Publishers/Deems Taylor Award for music-related journalistic writing. He's written about jazz and blues artists for *DownBeat, JazzTimes,* and *The Boston Globe,* and has voted in the Grammy Awards (2007–2020). Additionally, he's composed, recorded, and released two "Loose Caboose Band" CDs of original children's songs with his brother, Bill (*The Caboose is Loose* and *Mighty Big Broom,* the latter of which was honored with two first-voting-round Grammy nominations). He's also published a book on jazz, *Big Noise From Notre Dame: A History of the Collegiate Jazz Festival* (University of Notre Dame Press, 1986).

Joe holds an undergraduate degree from the University of Notre Dame, as well as graduate degrees from Boston University and the University of Iowa Writers' Workshop. When not scribbling down poems about daily life, the fascinating world around him, or his world travels, Joe runs a property management business, chases an occasionally-errant golf ball around the local public golf links at sunset (when the light glows best on the clouds in a dazzlingly-pure painted sky and deer start to slowly emerge from the surrounding woods), and continually tries to master Chuck Berry, B.B. King, and Scotty Moore riffs on acoustic and electric guitars.

Website:
www.josephkuhncareycreativeworks.com

www.ingramcontent.com/pod-product-compliance
Lightning Source LLC
Chambersburg PA
CBHW022014160426
43197CB00007B/432